First Facts®

ALL ABOUT MEDIA

FACT, FICTION, and OPINIONS:

THE DIFFERENCE BETWEEN ADS, BLOGS, NEWS REPORTS, and OTHER MEDIA

by BRIEN J. JENNINGS

CAPSTONE PRESS
a capstone imprint

First Facts Books are published by Capstone Press,
1710 Roe Crest Drive, North Mankato, Minnesota 56003
www.mycapstone.com

Library of Congress Cataloging-in-Publication Data is available on the Library of Congress website.
ISBN 978-1-5435-0222-0 (library binding)
ISBN 978-1-5435-0226-8 (paperback)
ISBN 978-1-5435-0230-5 (ebook pdf)

Editorial Credits:
Erika L. Shores, editor; Juliette Peters, designer;
Morgan Walters, media researcher; Kathy McColley, production specialist

Photo Credits:
Alamy: Agencja Fotograficzna Caro, 5, Hero Images Inc., 15, Jeff Greenberg 6 of 6, 17;
Shutterstock: Africa Studio, 11, Akkaradet Bangchun, (tv) 12, Anutr Yossundara, 20, Artur. B, (icons) design element, Charts and Table, Cover, Denis Rozhnovsky, (billboard) 12, Di Studio, (blog) 12, Duplass, left Cover, Mat Hayward, 7, MITstudio, (drink) 12, MK photograp55, 14, Rawpixel.com, 21, Roman Tiraspolsky, 13, Supphachai Salaeman, design element throughout, VGstockstudio, 19, vmalafeevskiy, (fast food) 12, wavebreakmedia, 9

Printed and bound in the USA.
010880S18

Table of Contents

All About Media

What do ads, **blogs**, and news reports have in common? They are types of media. Books, websites, movies, news reports, and **apps** are media as well. Media sends a message. An **audience** receives the message.

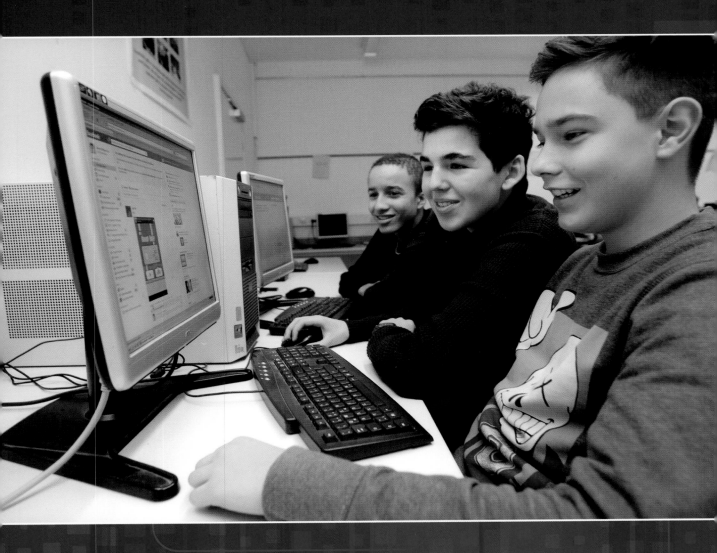

blog—a journal on the Internet; short for weblog
app—a program that is downloaded to computers and
    mobile devices; app is short for application
audience—people who hear, read, or see a message

5

Who is the audience for media messages? You are! So it's up to you to ask a lot of questions. Ask questions to figure out the media maker's **purpose**. Why was the message made? Understanding the purpose helps you know if the media's message is fact, fiction, or opinion.

purpose—the reason for which something is made or done

Media informs, entertains, and persuades. Media that informs includes facts. Facts are true. We check facts by finding **evidence**.

If media's purpose is to entertain, then it may be fiction. Fiction is not true. It is made up.

Sometimes media's purpose is to persuade. This type of media often includes opinions. An opinion is an idea or feeling about something. An opinion is not the same as a fact. We can't prove opinions are true.

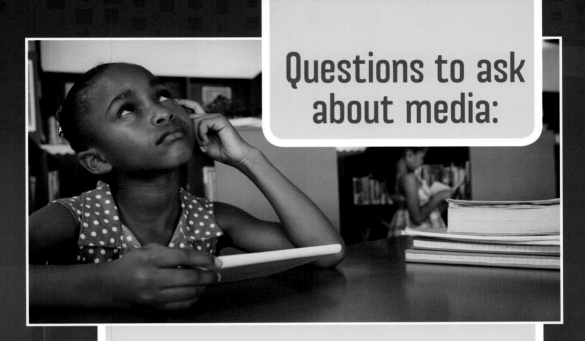

Questions to ask about media:

Who created the media?

Who is the audience for the media?

How does the author try to keep the audience's attention?

Why was the media made?

Does it give important information (inform)?

Does it tell a story, make you laugh, cry, or feel a certain way (entertain)?

Does it try to change your mind or convince you of something (persuade)?

evidence—information, items, and facts that help prove something to be true or false

9

Ads

Advertisements, or ads, are made to sell something. They're not fiction, and they're not always an opinion. The main purpose of an ad is to persuade or to get you to buy something. Ads also might try to change your mind about a topic or product.

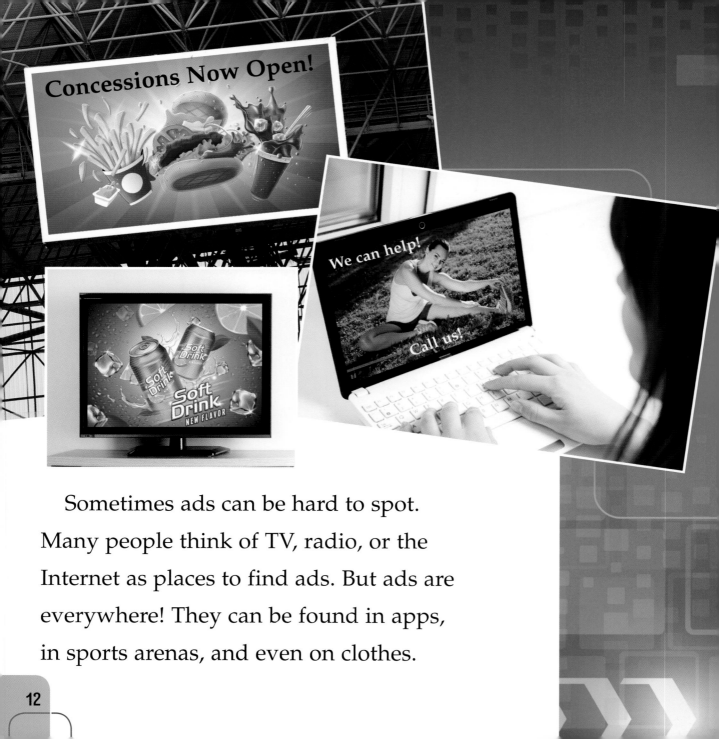

Sometimes ads can be hard to spot. Many people think of TV, radio, or the Internet as places to find ads. But ads are everywhere! They can be found in apps, in sports arenas, and even on clothes.

logo—a picture or a symbol that a company puts on its products

Blogs

A blog is a website people use to make an online journal. People who write or record blogs are called bloggers. Anyone can be a blogger. Some bloggers share real news events. Others share their thoughts, or opinions, about news events, games, toys, or other topics. You must check other sources before trusting that information on a blog is true.

Think About It!

Blog is short for weblog. Blogs can be fun to read or watch. But be sure to pay attention and think carefully about the information a blogger is sharing. Where is the information coming from? Is it fact or opinion?

News Reports

News reports give the facts about events in your city, country, and the world. A news reporter's job is to write or tell a true account of the event. The reporter does this by answering six main questions—who, what, why, where, when, and how.

You need to think carefully about news reports you read or hear. Sometimes stories that appear to be news reports are really ads. Other times news reports won't include all the facts or both sides of a story. Ask yourself whether or not the news report left out information. Did the report only tell one side of the story? Did the news report include the writer's opinions?

social media—websites that let people share words, pictures, and videos with other people

19

Everything In Between

You see and use media every day. People share opinions with friends on social media. People visit websites to watch videos. Media messages are everywhere. Sometimes it can be hard to tell the difference between fact, fiction, and opinion. TV shows and games can be entertaining and have ads. It's easy for bloggers to mix facts and opinions. That's why it's important for you to question what you read, hear, or see in the media.

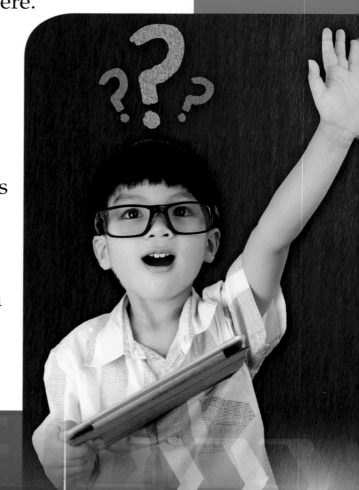

TRY IT! Look at some ads in magazines or online. Imagine something you'd like to sell, like a new toy. Write an ad for it. Who is your audience? How will you get your audience to pay attention? Will you use pictures? If you video your ad, will you use music?

Glossary

advertisement (ad-vuhr-TYZ-muhnt)—a notice that calls attention to a product or an event

app (APP)—a program that is downloaded to computers and mobile devices; app is short for application

audience (AW-dee-uhns)—people who hear, read, or see a message

blog (BLOG)—a journal on the Internet; short for weblog

evidence (EV-uh-duhnss)—information, items, and facts that help prove something to be true or false

logo (LOH-goh)—a symbol of a company's brand

persuade (pur-SWADE)—to change a person's mind, or to make a person believe something

purpose (PURP-iss)—the reason for which something is made or done

social media (SOH-shuhl MEE-dee-uh)—websites that let people share words, pictures, and videos with other people

Read More

Mooney, Carla. *Asking Questions About How the News Is Created.* Asking Questions About Media. Ann Arbor, Mich.: Cherry Lake Publishing, 2016.

Rustad, Martha E. H. *Learning About Fact and Opinion.* Media Literacy for Kids. North Mankato, Minn.: Capstone Press, 2015.

Woolf, Alex. *Let's Think About the Internet and Social Media.* Let's Think About. Chicago: Heinemann Library, 2015.

Internet Sites

Use FactHound to find Internet sites related to this book:

Visit *www.facthound.com*

Just type in 9781543502220 and go.

Check out projects, games and lots more at
www.capstonekids.com

Critical Thinking Questions

1. What is the purpose of a news report?

2. If you had your own blog, what would you write about and why?

3. Describe the difference between a fact and an opinion.

Index